Leaders

Enhance Your Capabilities in Leadership Communication,
Team Building, and Employee Management

*(Demonstrated Strategies and Techniques That Define the
Authentic Leader Within You)*

Stewart Butler

TABLE OF CONTENT

Structure of Hierarchy

Leadership concepts may have evolved beyond their former hierarchical structure. The evolution of leadership is incorporating distributed activity. The foundation of distributed leadership is education and...It is the consequence of a network of interconnected individuals as opposed to the action of a single individual.

Leadership opportunities are now accessible to individuals who were previously excluded. Exemplify the conviction that knowledge and sway are dispersed across the entire organization, as opposed to being centralized in the possession of a limited few individuals.

For instance, WL Gore, an authority on outdoor apparel, opted for a distributed leadership framework characterized by a "lattice" formation.

Emerging due to the development of sophisticated web technology are novel forms of organizations predicated on mass collaboration. While self-organizing bodies have founders and leaders, their approach to leadership is distinct from that of conventional enterprises. They safeguard the principles, values, and ethos of the communities that they are tasked with serving. Holacracy is a contemporary paradigm of non-hierarchical leadership. Based on their functions and objectives, departments are organized into circles and subcircles in this model. Consistently convening, sub-circles execute independent decision-making with the organization's objectives in consideration (the largest, all-encompassing circle). Sub-circle representatives are assigned to serve as intermediaries and ensure that the needs of the circles under their sub-responsibility are fulfilled. Individuals in this model possess authority and accountability, and all employ leadership abilities to govern themselves.

Becoming a More Effective Leader: A Guide

Extreme shifts in perceptions of leadership have occurred at both the academic and organizational levels. It is widely acknowledged that top-down, autocratic leadership is essentially unnecessary in the current business environment, characterized by rapid change and the pursuit of success in a highly competitive and ever-more global market.

Among these, the presence of well-informed leaders is particularly advantageous. Respected and revered, these leaders are authorities in their respective fields. They possess credibility and are deserving of reverence and compliance. This significantly facilitates the ability of these leaders to motivate and inspire their followers.

Good leaders must be ethical, culturally sensitive, flexible, and adaptable to retain the trust of their stakeholders and employees. Leaders of today and tomorrow will collaborate, deliberate, and delegate authority to optimize their performance, that of their teams, and that of the organization.

According to Captain Mark Brouker, an advocate for the U.S. Navy, leaders benefit from understanding the potential dangers of their position to the people they supervise and implementing strategies to mitigate that danger. For instance, business administrators determine the compensation and job security of employees. A good leader should, therefore, strive to establish trust, be approachable, and convey to others that making mistakes and learning from them is acceptable.

According to Goffee and Jones, effective leaders generally possess the following qualities:

Self-awareness.

A sense of comfort with their origins.

The capacity to adapt while ascending the corporate hierarchy while preserving their authenticity.

Authentic leaders demonstrate qualities such as integrity, accountability, and fortitude. Bill George, an authority on management from Harvard, asserts that they do not attempt to transform themselves into the type of leaders they consider themselves to be. They maintain their loyalty to their true selves.

They cultivate enduring relationships with others, exercise self-control, and lead with intention, significance, and values. As per George's assertion, authentic leaders establish authentic organizations that can deliver enduring value to their investors and clients while also being less susceptible to mismanagement and corruption.

The Methods Relating to Business Leadership

Our organization continues to operate in a world where the words "modification" dictate acquiring new projects. Leaders of organizations no longer have the luxury of determining whether or not they will unquestionably implement changes; rather, they must determine how they will enhance their organizations to survive in a constantly evolving environment. A current issue with Business Total complete week records: "... there is no doubt that the business environment has undergone a significant technological transformation." The resources administrators presently employed with great success are undergoing revision without exception; all of my most egregious errors were discovered due to my transition occurring too slowly.

The adjustment process may easily involve consideration to potentially establish the optimal organization. A recently published book, "Modification or Even Passage on," explains why the odds are, in fact, nine to one, that individuals will not modify their behavior even when confronted with the possibility of failing prematurely due to poor patterns. Entrepreneurs under constant pressure to respond to a rapidly changing world must have the means to overcome various obstacles and safeguard brand-new endeavors so they are never apprehended prematurely.

The Investigation

Numerous accounts and experiences of promoting change provided by individuals spearheading global organizational enhancements were compiled for this purpose. The sentiments expressed in their accounts were recorded and incorporated with additional research inquiries regarding adjustment and impact. Throughout this process, the inquiries were consistently presented for feedback and responses at seminars and with consumers with expertise in leading adjustment.

When an investigation identified a successful and recurring strategy for directing change, this was documented as a "pattern." Simply as its name implies, a pattern documents a procedure that has occurred repeatedly. Christopher Alexander documented effective layout practices in the architecture profession using this method of style chronicling. His emphasis on practical solutions rather than completely novel and distinctive ones was motivated by his observation that contemporary cities and buildings lacked the elegance of bygone eras. Alexander explained that, in contrast to a concept or deliberate strategy that may or may not be operational, a design delineates a possibility that has been effectively implemented across numerous scenarios. A particular concept outlines a successful resolution to a recurring issue, but integrating them into what is known as a "create language" provides a tool for managing unquestionably complex problems, such as overseeing correction in an administration.

This research study on business adjustment has identified 58 dependable strategies, or concepts, that individuals at all levels within an organization can implement to facilitate change. The compilation gives adjustment brokers a lexicon to engage in constructive discussions concerning their concerns and alternatives because every entry is unique.

Collaborating with change representatives, be they younger, brand-new staff members or the chief executive officer, can frequently induce a sense of "powerlessness in the forerunners" due to the inherent difficulty and protracted nature of altering individuals' perspectives. On the contrary, this research demonstrates that leaders who employ designs to address challenges during the process are significantly more successful at generating "buy-in." They execute a change campaign that strategically involves and informs stakeholders about the aspects of the process that they aim to modify.

The Initial Factor

The design delineating the individual who will spearhead the transformation is called an "Authorized Evangelist." This is because the distributor of the change must not only have faith in the novel concept and enthusiasm for its execution to inspire others to follow suit. This viewpoint will undoubtedly accompany the inventor due to the inevitable annoyances that arise during the process. According to the remodeling pioneers interviewed, a genuine understanding of the significance of their principles for their controls is essential before inspiring others.

Effectively employing a design entails recognizing the suitable context for its implementation and the resulting outcomes of treatment. The Evangelist design prevents one from appearing overly enthusiastic because while enthusiasm may inspire individuals to receive information, persistence may alienate them.

Applied Religion

Romans 12:2 in the Bible says, "Be transformed by the renewing of your mind, and do not conform to the pattern of this world." You will then be able to evaluate God's good, pleasing, and perfect will.

To put it simply, this lyric is about turning away from the noise of this world. There are so many voices, all of them vying for your attention. You must put everyone else in the background and create patterns to fulfill your destiny.

Applied Faith: Self-assured belief in the integrity, worth, or reliability of a person, concept, or item.

A viewpoint that is not supported by tangible evidence or reason.

Napoleon Hill went on to describe it as a mental condition exclusive to individuals who have mastered the ability to seize total and complete control of their thoughts. The mindset allows your thoughts to be free of fear and concentrate on more desirable objectives. He said there are two ways to employ faith: when applied incorrectly, it causes anxiety, ultimately resulting in failure. When applied properly, it can yield great benefits.

It's crucial to define and interpret applied faith in your unique way. You must have faith in your interpretation to internalize it and bring it to life to help you reach your objectives.

Many users encounter failure when attempting to apply this technology to their everyday lives, rather than failure in the sense that it is defined. Because it's one thing to say the words; it's another to be able to believe them. Many people take their faith for granted and consider themselves religious. But the belief may only be a habit of thinking rather than a true belief. The individual must demonstrate their faith in something greater than themselves to validate their belief.

Faith in a power greater than oneself, whether nature, the world, or God.

What you believe that Infinite Intelligence to be is entirely up to you. It is also up to you to decide whether you believe infinite intelligence serves a purpose. And that He gave you the power to fulfill your destiny at the same time that He created you.

You can accomplish anything if you imagine this faith, gather your conviction, and act fervently on it.

To put it another way, if you quit your negative self-talk and your lack of belief that stems from "I can't," "It'll never happen," or "It's impossible, "Faith encourages us to think that we can achieve our goals once we give up on the idea that we "can't." Barack Obama, the president of the United States, is a prime example of the strength of faith; throughout his presidential campaign, he used the phrase "Yes we can!"

He did. Two times.Despite all of his difficulties, setbacks, and obstacles. He achieved his objective. It all starts with believing in yourself and using your faith to accomplish your objectives.

Thinking Outside the Box

"For we are God's workmanship, made in Christ Jesus to accomplish good deeds, which God planned for us to accomplish beforehand" (Ephesians 2:10

Being a leader will allow you to face hardship, making you more resilient and equipped to guide groups through operations with sincere concern for your and your team's growth. When you witness your colleagues' growth, it is during these times that you become aware of the true influence of your work.

This drive to achieve sometimes coincides with the leader's persistence, bringing revelation and a learning experience. It doesn't matter how hard you work to progress; what matters is how open a person is to receiving guidance. This directly relates to how a leader inspires people, gives them credit for their accomplishments, and supports them when they make mistakes.

Rewarding a worker because of their job stability was one of the previously listed factors. In this case, a tenure-track employee or one worried about losing their position might choose a reward that acknowledges their commitment to the organization. This kind of incentive would have to suit the person's culture, considering their age, gender, and individual characteristics.[3]

Since funding outside of the regular budget may be scarce, a leader needs to consider more comparable approaches to ensure associate satisfaction at or near the same level. At this point, the leader's thoughts about compensation, strategy, and budget converge with prayer.

The recommended reward for this kind of person would be an increase in paid time off beyond their allocated hours. Giving a tenured employee, for instance, an extra hour or so of paid time off or longer lunches or breaks might be appropriate as an exception.

This associate should be aware that this recognition is due to their ongoing commitment to the organization, demonstrated by their attendance and unique contributions to the team. It should be clarified that the company values the associate's commitment and wants them to know how important they are to the team's and the organization's overall success.

The employee's example of professional development was the subject of the second criterion mentioned above. This associate should receive a reward that aligns with their desire to succeed and advance to the next level of their career.

An effective leader in tune with the Holy Spirit can discern the talents and areas in which a worker would like to grow while seizing the organization's possibilities to advance these abilities. It could be possible to develop and bring these skills to life with the help of specific programs or materials. In this case, the leader might highlight the capabilities and offer the chance for professional or personal development as a reward for demonstrating these abilities.

After receiving this reward, the colleague should speak with the leader and outline their professional goals. Now that they have this knowledge, the manager can suggest more assignments and positions to help the worker pursue their dream of a higher salary.

These kinds of awards wouldn't be material; instead, they would be a first step toward the employee moving up the corporate ladder. Workers will also value their boss's consideration of their individual goals, whether within or outside the organization.

It was discovered that males who believed management cared about their wellbeing had significantly more faith in the senior manager than those who believed management showed little concern for them. Put another way, the senior supervisor also stood or fell based on the management's commitment to people's wellbeing. A similar difference was also observed regarding trust in the direct supervisor.

Employees had greater faith in their immediate supervisor when they perceived management to be concerned about their wellbeing than when they did not.

But there was one significant distinction. The senior supervisor did not stand or fall as firmly as the manager did, even if he did it by these terms. There was less difference between the positive and negative groups in the eyes of the supervisors. Again, for the direct supervisor, this difference was less.

Power, Supervisors, and Managers

Consequently, we concluded that while the same criterion was applied to evaluate managers, senior supervisors, and middle managers, it was not applied equally.

In summary:

Initially, the worker assessed the manager based on a basic standard: did the management truly care about the worker's wellbeing?

Second, this criterion was applied less strictly the lower the manager was in the organization and the less powerful he was. On the other hand, the condition was enforced more strictly the more powerful the manager.

These results indicate a connection between power and the standards employees evaluate their supervisors. Indeed, it is clear that employees' standards for judging management align with those for determining power. We were astonished when this relationship initially occurred to us at the Human Resources laboratory since it seemed unworthy of a group of liberal social scientists to come to such a result.

Reexamining the situation, however, reveals that authority and the standards by which employees evaluate their supervisors are related. In the job, power is everything. A manager or supervisor uses his power when he gives a subordinate instructions.

No manager can act arbitrarily just because he is a higher-ranking employee or receives compensation or any other reason. A boss can request that someone "deliver" something, but only if he truly cares.

Keeping this in mind, yet another crucial outcome became apparent. The immediate supervisor of Mine H (the high-trust mine) was the subject of a significant disparity in trust between the positive and negative groups. This discrepancy suggested that the immediate supervisor was subject to a comparatively strict application of the criterion by which the employees judged their power in Mine H.

This could be verified by examining the types of choices that a supervisor may make. He could handle any issue, even unpaid leave and financial advances. Therefore, it would appear that the degree to which a supervisor is empowered to oversee their subordinates is correlated with high levels of managerial trust.

Mine F provided evidence of the opposite. Of the six mines under consideration, the one with the lowest level of faith in management was the black supervisor, and there was very little difference in trust between the positive and negative groups. Put another way, the black supervisor on Mine F was scarcely evaluated based on the standard by which power was evaluated. The black supervisor was not seen as a symbol of authority or management but as another decent black coworker. This indicates that management was not trusted when the immediate supervisor was not viewed as powerful.

The characteristics of Parker

Glenn Parker, who has dedicated his professional life to studying teams, created the twelve traits of successful teams. The group will examine some of these traits for the rest of the afternoon and tomorrow.

Explicit Goal

Casualty

Engagement

Paying attention

Calm Conflicts

Consensus Choices

Honest Communication

Clearly defined roles and tasks

Joint Leadership

Style of External Relations Variety

Self-Evaluation

Explicit Goal

Each of us values having objectives or a distinct purpose on a personal level. According to seminal research, just 3% of Yale grads established goals, but that 3% went on to earn more money and achieve greater success than the other 97% combined.

There are a few elements to consider when defining objectives for leaders, and SMART PPP is a great acronym to help you keep them in mind. This acronym stands for timeliness, specificity, measurableness, attainability, and realisticness. Additionally, objectives have to be personalized for every team member, stated positively, and all of them have to be Put on paper at a location that you and the team can visit frequently.

Creating an action plan to reach your goals can be highly helpful after you and your team have established some objectives.

Participation and Informality

The atmosphere on high-performing teams is usually easygoing, cozy, and carefree. No overt evidence of boredom or tension is present. Teams love to get together since they get along well with one another and laugh and joke around a lot. The way people are seated can help with this. The ideal seating arrangement is typically in a circle; the worst is usually in a typical classroom.

Paying attention

Effective listening strategies high-performance team members use include questioning, paraphrasing, and summarizing to extract ideas. The most effective way to separate successful teams from ineffective ones is via listening. Sadly, there is less action and more lip paid to it.

A crucial characteristic of any team member is the capacity for attentive listening. By listening, you can demonstrate your interest in what the other person says and gain insight into their perspective. Regretfully, hearing impairments are a prevalent concern for everyone.

Our gaze strayed.

The true meaning of what is being conveyed is lost on us.

We step on other people's words and interrupt them.

We miss what is said because we are too busy planning what to say next.

Use the three active listening procedures to enhance your listening abilities. Nonverbal Communication. A forward body tilt, head nod, eye contact, and alert look convey listening. Indications or invites. These cues, such as uh-huh, OK, yes, or continue, draw attention to ourselves and extend an invitation to speak further.

Clarification of the previous remarks. We can accomplish this in a few different ways, such as by posing queries, summarizing previous remarks, or crafting our paraphrase of the message.

However, the fact that their compensation is determined by considering all relevant factors, including their productivity, experience, and work hours, makes it equitable. Equity can refer to everything reasonable and strikes a balance given all the factors at play, not only remuneration.

Thus, equity and equality are not the same. It functions similarly to a scale that measures more than simply the outcome. Equitable remuneration for those who give more needs to be provided via the equity scale, even though opportunity and access are equal.

But taking the big picture into account is essential to make it equitable. It may be about anything; it's not just about the money. Moreover, equity and equality are not the same. It functions similarly to a scale considering factors other than the final product. Even though accessibility and opportunity are equal, equality requires that the individual contributing more be paid more.

Equity is crucial in the workplace because of this. People are inspired to give it their all rather than "quietly quit." Individuals who work harder and generate greater output should be compensated for it. If there is no equity, why would someone make an effort if they don't perceive any gain or benefit? At this point, "quiet quitting" occurs—people simply cease doing their hardest. Therefore, fostering equity in the workplace ensures that people's extra effort is recognized and appreciated.

Equity in the workplace is vital because it inspires people to perform better and be more productive. Furthermore, we are not interested in "quiet quitters" or those who gradually stop working without officially giving up. Due to a lack of fairness in the workplace, which can cause people to become overly sensitive to the thought of favoring some people over others, this is a serious problem in the modern economy.

But no two people are alike. Employees who work more and deliver better should be compensated for it. People will start to lose motivation, and their chances of quitting quietly increase considerably if they believe their hard work will not be appreciated. Equity in the workplace is crucial because it demonstrates to employees that their additional effort is valued. They feel appreciated and receive the acknowledgment they are due.

Equity counts when it comes to leadership. You are in the spotlight as a leader, setting the tone for the entire organization. If leaders are making varying degrees of contributions, this discrepancy needs to be addressed. Even if a leader contributes less, it sends the wrong message and creates a harmful precedent when they are given preference over other leaders. For this reason, leadership equity is essential. Simply put, managers are no more likely to quietly depart than the employees they oversee.

To put it another way, morale can be severely damaged if your group, business, or organization notices that certain leaders are receiving higher compensation or recognition but making less of an impact. The remainder of the organization receives a negative message from this unfair treatment. There are two types of people in leadership, particularly in middle management: those who see it as a job and those who give it their all. Rewarding people who come and go in the same manner as those who put in a full day's work is unfair. The department, if not the entire organization, is usually in the hands of those who embody their leadership role. Let's discuss the distinctions between equity and equality. Consider a manager who views their position as merely that—a position. They don't put in any extra effort; they are just involved during working hours. A pleasant work environment won't be created if they continue to be handled and portrayed in the same manner as a leader dedicated to their profession. Since most workers in a company don't have leadership or management positions, it's critical to foster an environment that supports them.

Equity is important in leadership, not only for the leaders themselves but also for the organization. Leaders must model equity in their behavior to prevent problems like low morale and silent resignation. Employee loyalty and brand confidence increase when they feel valued for their work.

Since equitable treatment isn't always the same as fair treatment, treating people differently is OK. Equity rewards those who work more, perform better, and complete tasks more effectively. This fosters respect and acknowledgment. In this sense, performance is the basis for praise, admiration, rewards, and remuneration rather than just title. By taking this action, leaders can prevent an environment with a high personnel turnover rate and a lack of effort.

Step 5: Develop your craft.

Being a master is a prerequisite for being a leader. Only if you are skilled at what you do will people respect you. But how does one become a master? I shall list the essential actions to becoming an authority in your industry, even though there isn't a single correct answer to this query. They should be viewed as guidelines rather than regulations because they are not in a certain order.

Where are you at this moment?

You must assess your current situation first. What areas of your current knowledge are you almost an expert in? You may be already proficient in your current field or very near to being proficient, so it will be easy to expand and advance your competence. Learning anything completely new is far more time-consuming and difficult than taking this much simpler way. However, you must ensure that the work you are performing now still piques your interest. This phase was discussed in a previous chapter, but choosing a path that inspires you is crucial.

You will need to determine what piques your interest if the work you are doing now doesn't. This needs to be your top concern. Whichever path you select, your area of expertise ought to inspire you. You won't have the motivation and vigor required for significant endeavors until then.

Instead of attempting to correct flaws, concentrate on your strengths.

We were taught to know a little bit about everything in school. This method saves you time in becoming an expert at one item, although it doesn't appear that good initially. In this manner, you will never become a master, only mediocre. After determining what truly interests you, focusing on this item is the next stage. Put this topic front and center and clear your mind of any distractions. You will only set yourself up for failure if you try to study too much at once and overwhelm yourself.

Try using computer programs for your models if you have a strong sense of design and want to become a successful architect but aren't very good at, for instance, drawing. In this manner, you can capitalize even more on your abilities and avoid wasting time on those holding you back. Another option is to ask coworkers for assistance with your designs and offer to repay the favor by offering guidance in an area of expertise. It all boils down to realizing that you are a fallible human being. Spending time on something you are interested in and where you have the opportunity to excel is a better use of your time.

Prioritize learning above money.

Many people make the error of becoming engrossed in the egotistical pursuit of an idealized life. Instead of considering potential, they judge opportunities and labor based on money. Rather, you should prioritize learning above all else. In the long term, this is the much superior option. You can make money indefinitely. Your time invested in creating it cannot. According to author Malcolm Gladwell, proficiency in a given profession requires roughly 10,000 hours of practice. If all you do is chase after money, you will never have this much time for your hobbies.

Invest in your education.

Have you noticed that I said to educate yourself? This is because you can learn almost anything on your own these days. Even the most distant subjects can be studied at home using internet resources like Khan Academy (an iTunes course on neurosurgery, for example). The best part is that it's nearly always free. No lecturer will ever force you to take a final test, and you are free to study only interesting subjects. Online learning is a truly wonderful method to spend your free time doing something worthwhile that will advance your profession.

Utilize your history

A lot of us are desperate to get away from our history. But your past will always be with you unless scientists develop a technology that lets you erase memories. This is your chance, as you should perceive it. Even the darkest moments in life can be seen as hidden blessings. In life, a lot of doors only open when another closes. Following the failure of two earlier websites, Mark Zuckerberg developed Facebook. He could only determine what worked after the grueling process of seeing what didn't. You might be surprised by yourself if you look for ways that your history can improve your present.

It all comes down to attitude.

Everything that occurs in your inner world is reflected in the outside world. If you see the world negatively, all you will see is terrible. Opportunities and friends will find you if you take on a more upbeat and happy outlook. The law of attraction is a true phenomenon. You may also say everything is meaningless; you get what you put in. Positivity is crucial if you want to become an expert in your field. You can't allow setbacks or failure to defeat you. Standing up will be difficult at first, but if you can make it a habit, you will eventually be able to do it without much difficulty.

Everybody is different from birth.

Even if you have an identical twin, no one else is exactly like you. This regulation is comparable to concentrating on your strengths instead of attempting to correct flaws. Being accepted is overvalued. Discover your true uniqueness and learn to love it. The quickest route to sadness and depression is to try to be someone else. Because of this, I dedicated an entire chapter to values. Establish yours and defend them. Though they may be critical, people will still respect you.

Increase the variety of your contributions.

Imagine what would happen to your outlook if all you could think about was the news and TV. The number of worldwide tragedies and mishaps can leave you feeling overwhelmed.

Conversely, you don't want to read the same book 200 times. You need a variety of inputs to achieve the best results. What is meant by that? Read works in many genres. Enjoy a variety of musical genres. Experiment with everything. Take the scenic road through life and stray off the usual path.

It's never too late.

If you think, "That sounds helpful and interesting, but I'm too old to make changes," after reading this book, keep in mind that Colonel Sanders, the inventor of KFC, made his first million at the age of 65. You're never too old or too late to take action. A lot of individuals just get lost while traveling. They let the voice of other people's knowledge to overpower their intuition. This is the point of danger. They make the wrong decisions because other people instruct them on what to do and how to think. You must listen to that voice and follow your calling to become a master.

STARTING AT THE BACK

"Leading from behind and putting people ahead is preferable, especially when you celebrate success when good things happen. When there's danger, you lead the charge. People will then value your leadership at that point.

Certain leaders require attention. They simply think about themselves and chase after glory. They are the ones who attempt solo ascents to the highest peaks, which inevitably results in the longest fall. Leaders who prioritize their team and see the importance of leading from the rear will reach the same summit together and be able to save one another from falling off the edge.

I use the expression "leading from the back" as my motto or catchphrase for all my leadership endeavors. It's easy to stand before them and give them instructions. It's challenging to lead your team from the rear while assisting them in becoming future leaders and individuals who will help you realize your vision.

The analogy used to describe traditional administrative leadership was a CEO at the top, employees at the base, and middle management making up the remaining positions in a pyramid.

Subsequently, the field of customer relations emerged, putting forth the idea of an inverted pyramid where the firm is at the base and the customers are at the top. Although not the main area of focus, customer relations has influenced leadership approaches in related corporate domains. This lends credence to the idea that the client is always right. Nonetheless, I suggest a fresh visual style for leadership.

Figure 1: Leadership Styles: Conventional versus Modern

If you're more mathematically minded, think of a wave or a sinusoidal function to get what I mean when I say "leading from the back."

Figure 2: Front-facing vs rear-facing leadership

Leadership is a wave; there are moments when you should lead from the front and others when you should lead from the back. You are always changing from where you lead because of particular circumstances. A good leader is someone who accepts a little more than their fair share of responsibility and a little less than their fair share of credit, according to the well-known quote by John Maxwell.10 As a result, in the event of a mishap, the team leader assumes full responsibility while shielding the group from criticism.

However, the team leader takes a backseat when things are going well and lets their members enjoy the recognition. There will be more explanation of the precise circumstances in which you should apply both leading tactics. This is what it means to lead from the rear. I can attest from personal experience that this is your toolkit's most effective and difficult leadership style.

Putting Together Your Toolkit

Because you overcame every obstacle you encountered, you are here. It'll force you to use all of the knowledge and abilities you've acquired to expand your toolkit and excel as a leader. Building your toolbox or assembling leadership resources to tackle daily obstacles is invaluable. Methods, knowledge, abilities, tactics, and experiences are all considered leadership tools that can be applied to any circumstance.

I'll give leaders knowledge and resources to address a range of difficult situations they might encounter in their line of work. You will be more prepared to handle everyday setbacks and leadership challenges if you can expand your toolkit.

Remember that not every tool is appropriate for every case and that just because it has worked in the past doesn't guarantee it will do so. It all boils down to assessing the circumstances and attempting one approach while remaining flexible to employing several. An effective leader can only learn which tools work in different scenarios by constant trial and error.

Chapter 4: Your Approaches to Leadership

Leaders influence and motivate people to make constructive changes that enhance the status quo!

What many distinct leadership philosophies exist?

Robert Blake and Jane Mouton's Leadership Grid outlines five different leadership philosophies.

Four leadership philosophies are outlined in the Situational Leadership Theory Model, which Paul Hersey and Ken Blanchard created.

It comes down to three main types, in my opinion: delegating, discussing, and directing.

Employing the right leadership style will assist individuals in changing and improving their effectiveness.

Do you know how to use all three techniques well?

Managing Leadership Attitude

A leader explains to an individual or group what adjustments are required and why. The leader specifically outlines the objective, strategy, and timeframe.

Your objective is to ensure that every customer support representative is an expert user of the new program in all respects.

Plan: There are five things I want you to do.

Deadline: By the end of the fourth quarter, this must be finished and implemented.

Most communication between a leader and an employee is one-way. "Do you understand the instructions?" is the only feedback the leader seeks.

The guiding method is suitable when people lack the necessary skills and will to effect the necessary change. People need and expect clear instructions on what to do in this case and how to do it.

Talking About Leadership Style

More than 2,000 years ago, Socrates discovered that asking the proper questions was more important for effective leadership than providing answers. The most effective leaders pose inquiries that compel and inspire others to determine what is required to address issues and seize opportunities. Their inquiries center on the objective, schedule, and timeframe.

Goal: What is our aim? How can we take action that has never been taken before? What ought to be our objective? What do we hope to achieve?

Plan: What steps are necessary? What challenges are you expecting? How are we going to get over them? Who is the most suitable candidate for each job? What was learned from the last implementation?

Deadline: How long will it take to reasonably finish this change endeavor? How will that deadline affect people's behavior? What additional things could affect this deadline?

Two-way communication occurs between a leader and their followers. It calls for cooperation and openness. Leaders spend much time listening, facilitating the conversation and providing insightful questions.

The conversation technique is appropriate when people are willing to change and have some experience and skills. In planning and making decisions, they might offer insights and suggestions.

The Leadership Style of Delegation

Effective leaders empower skilled individuals to set their objectives, schedules, and deadlines. They push and strain individuals to decide what needs to change and how best to make those changes.

Effective leaders need regular reports on large-scale change projects to ensure the right progress is being made.

When individuals are capable and motivated to change the status quo, delegating is a suitable approach.

Which Style Is Appropriate?

The ideal style isn't singular.

Every style has its proper place and uses, depending on the circumstances.

The most effective leaders assess the situation by considering pertinent elements, including people's knowledge, abilities, motivation, and willingness to adapt.

When someone lacks the necessary training or expertise, begin by providing guidance. As individuals acquire expertise and understanding, including them via dialogue and subsequently assigning tasks is optimal.

Leaders employ a blend of approaches in certain circumstances. For instance, they can employ directing and discussing styles when setting goals and coming up with a plan.

They change and adopt a new style if the one they are using isn't effective.

Employing the right leadership style fosters learning, development, and increased independence in others.

In brief

Things to keep in mind

Every circumstance is different. Make sure your leadership approach is appropriate for the circumstances.

Most leaders have a "go-to" style that they frequently employ. It's critical to expand your skill set and master all three leadership philosophies.

Being in the correct setting is always a factor in providing effective leadership.

Project Start-Up

Don't neglect to start the project! The starting stage offers the best chance of producing success. This is the ideal time to set up your project for success. It is now, not later that you should completely engage your team and achieve clarity of purpose. Consider this: you wouldn't jump off a rooftop without first checking your surroundings, would you? You wouldn't likely leap from a rooftop, but what about diving into a swimming pool? Would you dive in if you didn't know the splash zone, impact area, and depth? [Spring Break swimming events are not included.] Superheroes never jump without first looking. Projects, rooftops, and pools all need to be respected. Unless you're busy avoiding death rays, gunshots, or drunks, of course, don't let a friend, boss, or beverage dictate your decisions. In such instances, making a poor decision is preferable to doing nothing and taking a senseless beating.

Superheroes, above all, always take the lead before they jump. Nobody is ever asked to do something they wouldn't do themselves. Leaders influence other people's ideas and behaviors; they are neither observers, followers, or dictators. Define the project, outline its boundaries, and investigate any working restrictions during the project start phase of the project management process (also known as the Superhero's Success System). Assumptions that affect the project's outcome, whether correct or not, will be made, such as the amount of time and resources needed. It is your responsibility to encourage candid dialogue among all parties involved. Using this stage to foster courteous and fruitful relationships, a good leader effectively harvests the wisdom of the stakeholders, guiding others toward Clarity, Action, Purpose, and Enthusiasm.

Before beginning the planning phase, six crucial questions must be addressed. (Recall that our method raises more questions than it answers.)

1. Goal: Clearly state what the initiative will accomplish, enhance, lessen, or alter. Tell us how you plan to measure progress. Verify that the goal statement has the support of all important stakeholders. Assess the goal's

realisticness for yourself (and ask others to do the same). Establish any time limits to establish a controlled sense of urgency. You're undoubtedly aware that this is a modification of the "SMART" goal structure based on research.

2. Goals: How will this objective be accomplished? Which plans, techniques, or methods will be applied? Astute leaders understand that there are usually several approaches to accomplish any given task. As mentioned in Mastermind, select a course of action from your Action List that meets the project's objectives and limitations.

3. Stakeholders: Who will be a part of this undertaking? A stakeholder is, by definition, anyone who has an impact on

or is affected by a project. Many problems can be anticipated, prevented, or lessened by considering each stakeholder group's expectations, participation, and authority, as Problems are Predictable in Leading High-Stakes Adventures explains. Academics believe initiatives are successful when important stakeholders are significantly satisfied. (Sorry!) Your project is doomed from the start if you don't know who the important stakeholders are or how they will determine success.

4. Assumptions - Every project has some, some big, some little; some are observed, some are not; some are true, and some are as absurd as a duck's butt covered in chrome plating. List all of

your assumptions; the more you exclude, the greater the danger. Do you think that suppliers will provide what is specified? that companies will answer questions? and that your distant colleagues are just as concerned as you are? Although there is an infinite list of potential dangers, many can be avoided, lessened, or anticipated by accepting assumptions. Raise an enlightening question to each stakeholder group: "What are our working assumptions?" Finally, don't presume that everyone involved is rational.

5. Triple Constraints refer to the project's time balance, resources, and scope. Negative outcomes happen when a project's capacity and desire aren't

balanced. Stakeholders' goals are "good, fast, and cheap," but opening the door to something "too good, too fast, and too cheap" is akin to witnessing a scary movie. Compared to project teams that have just enough time and resources to fulfill the ambitious expectations of the stakeholders, those that maintain flexibility in any or all three of the triple limitations are more capable, resilient, and have a much higher chance of success. To learn how to create triple constraint flexibility and set up your project for success, check out Even Superheroes Need a Plan's How "Slow" Should You Start.

6. Commitment - "Are we committed to success?" is crucial. They hired me

because, as a turnaround specialist, I frequently deal with hazy aims, unclear goals, disregarded presumptions, and confused limits. Apathy is what I find unbearable. People can't win if they don't care, meaning none of us can. The world's best strategy will fail without individuals genuinely caring about each other, the project, and the company. Superheroes require ardent companions!

Consider the initiation phase as the start of your iterative learning process. Be on your guard; evil exists both within and outside. Watch out for these typical (and sometimes lethal) villains:

● Errors of Omission: A common reason for project failure is a lack of awareness of the work necessary to succeed.

● Overoptimism: Have you ever observed that work appears easier the farther you are from it? It is also true in reverse. The harder the labor gets, the closer you get to it. Something feasible in a boardroom setting might not be achievable in the real world.

● Overcommitment: People who are driven (as well as their organizations) frequently overcommit. With the best intentions, a portfolio may be jeopardized by taking on too many tasks. Recall that there are limits to any system.

The Use of Emotional Intelligence at Work

Comprehending emotions and their importance is crucial for productive teamwork and human relations. Emotional intelligence (EQ) is a vital competency that enables people to effectively traverse intricate social dynamics, establish robust connections, and improve overall productivity in the workplace. their effects, and the significance of emotional intelligence in the workplace.

The True Nature of Feelings

Emotions are fundamentally complex and multidimensional psychological reactions that emerge in response to different stimuli, experiences, or circumstances. They influence our thoughts, deeds, and interactions with the environment around us, making them an essential component of the human experience. There is a vast range of emotions, from happiness, love, and contentment to fear, rage, and sadness. Each emotion is associated with a distinct set of behavioral patterns, cognitive functions, and physiological alterations.

Emotions are powerful forces that impact personal and professional domains; they are not just transient feelings. Emotions can influence judgment, ingenuity, problem-solving, and relationship formation with others.

Although emotions can benefit our well-being, they can also cause conflict and difficulties, particularly if they are not recognized, understood, or controlled.

Emotions' Effect on the Workplace

Emotions permeate the workplace and have a significant effect on both individual and group performance. Good feelings like excitement and contentment support a peaceful workplace, higher levels of motivation, and improved interpersonal connections. Conversely, negative feelings such as stress, resentment, and frustration can cause poor decision-making, low productivity, and strained team dynamics.

Moreover, feelings have the power to motivate workers and promote workplace happiness. People are more likely to be driven, devoted, and devoted to the company when they feel appreciated, acknowledged, and emotionally supported at work. On the other hand, a culture that suppresses feelings or encourages negativity can result in low employee morale, high employee turnover, and poor organizational performance.

Emotional Intelligence's Function

It becomes clear that emotional intelligence (EQ) is essential for negotiating the complex emotional terrain of the workplace. Emotional intelligence, first defined by psychologists Peter Salovey and John Mayer and later popularized by author Daniel Goleman, is the capacity to identify, comprehend, regulate, and utilize one's emotions and those of others. It includes a range of abilities that promote constructive emotional reactions, social interaction, and the development of relationships.

101 on Emotions: What Are They and Why Are They Important?

Emotions are the vivid threads that make up the complex fabric of the human experience. They influence how we see the world, direct our choices, and mold the core of who we are. Emotions orchestrate our reactions to the world around us, acting as the music and choreography in life's intricate dance. In this "Emotions 101" examination, we go deep into the essence of emotions and examine why they are so powerful and significant in our lives.

Revealing the True Nature of Feelings

Emotions are fundamentally the interior climate of the human spirit. They appear as responses to various events, ideas, and experiences—from the minute to the profound. Emotion is a complex phenomenon that involves physiological reactions, cognitive functions, and behavioral tendencies. It is not only a transient emotion.

Think about the feeling of joy, which is a vibrant, thrilling emotion that can elevate one's spirits. When something happy happens or is accomplished, the body may react by releasing chemicals that make you feel good. Concurrently, mental processes elicit feelings of happiness and satisfaction. In terms of behavior, joy might be shown as grins, giggles, or happy faces.

On the other hand, feelings such as dread can elicit a completely distinct range of reactions. The body may release stress hormones that prime us for a fight-or-flight reaction in response to a perceived threat. Fear may cause ideas of risk and caution in the brain. In terms of behavior, it may cause elevated heart rate, heightened awareness, and a propensity to back away from the perceived threat.

The Purpose of Feelings

Emotions perform significant roles that have changed throughout human history; they are more than just irrational mental oscillations. Fundamentally, emotions are signals that bring important information to our conscious awareness. They give us an understanding of our wants, needs, and worldviews.

Imagine a scenario when you come across someone with a kind smile and an amiable manner. You may have feelings of trust and comfort, which indicate that this relationship is probably secure and constructive. On the other hand, feelings of uneasiness or caution may surface in a setting where something feels strange or unpleasant, urging you to exercise caution and vigilance.

7 A RAIL TO Wrocław

In 2013, I was on a formal visit to Germany. Our itinerary for the extended weekend included trips to Poland and the Czech Republic. We had arranged a road trip to the Czech city of Prague. Prague is possibly the most picturesque city in all of Europe. During World War II, Prague was not devastated because the Nazis took control of it without resistance. It was carried out to prevent the potential for Europe to become the theater of another World War. We were going to Krakow, a Polish city, after exploring the lovely city of Prague. Why my friend had put Krakow on the itinerary was a mystery to me. Then, I learned from one of my acquaintances that Auschwitz, a concentration camp located in Krakow, was the largest. Since I love history so much, I was excited to visit the Auschwitz concentration camp.

The train ride from Prague to Krakow was an interesting trip. The train bore a lot of similarities to Indian trains. These locations were a part of the Soviet Union following World War II. I'm guessing that Indian train cars are equipped with USSR technology. There were six seats in a cabin. A young man from Canada made up the sixth participant in our group of five. I struck up a discussion with him by inquiring as to his whereabouts. "He was traveling to the Auschwitz concentration camp," he informed me. The majority of his ancestors perished in the concentration camp known as Auschwitz. Nazis attempted to kidnap and send his grandfather to a camp. However, his great-grandmother misrepresented his grandfather's age to the Nazis, saying he was just thirteen. Since only adults over the age of fourteen were housed in concentration camps, he was spared. All of his relatives were required to dig pits at the camp. They were buried alive in the holes once they were dug. They had to excavate their graves. I was completely shocked to hear this. In pursuit of safety after the Second World War, his grandfather immigrated to Canada. "One should study both Gandhi and Hitler. One will teach you how high a human being can reach, and another will teach you how low a human being can go," American philosopher Jim Rohn once said.

The trip from Krakow to Auschwitz was incredibly depressing and silent. There was grief and an unfavorable energy in the air. Ultimately, the concentration camp at Auschwitz claimed the lives of 1.1 million individuals. Jews were initially the object of bigotry, hostility, and extreme nationality. The quote, "If you don't know your history, then you will end up reliving your history," was the first item on display when we arrived at the concentration camp.

During World War II, people were transported to the camp by train; the weak among them were immediately separated and killed; the healthy were forced to labor in the camps; they were tortured; and human rights were violated. Ultimately, however, the hatred and violence claimed the lives of 75 million people.

My takeaway from the visit was that racism, hatred, and intolerance can only lead humanity to concentration camps. Reasonable people must speak out when they see signs of racism, hatred, and intolerance emerging to preserve humanity. I saw intricate engineering drawings of the camp's gas chambers, where many people were killed by using poisonous gas. For the first time, I felt ashamed to be an engineer.

The Key to Effective Leadership Is Not a Title

You may have been good at your work, but leading people requires a new level of abilities that you may or may not possess. Just because you've been chosen to lead a team of people doesn't imply you're good at it. You might be terrible at it.

I've seen terrible leaders, so I've never pondered how someone got chosen to lead a group of people in the world.

In actuality, you may be doubting your abilities right now. Maybe you feel like you've been thrown into an arena of honor without the owner's manual. Don't be discouraged; many leaders have felt the same way. The truth is that many managers and supervisors simply don't know how to lead well. They desperately need to develop skills in this area.

Here's how many leaders, managers, and supervisors typically begin their leadership journey: upper management gives them a title of authority, and that's about it. Their boss then expects them to figure out how to fix everything or eventually gain the hang of it, but not too soon.

My spouse received an invitation to manage a sizable, rapidly expanding vision center. She was thrilled about the position; the pay was excellent, the staff was friendly, but worst of all, no training was provided. You can only imagine how irritated she was on her first day, spent awkwardly attempting to learn how to operate the optical equipment, the cash register, and the entire process.

I know women can be "hinters," but her reaction when she got inside the car spoke volumes! As she sat down, the tears streaming down her face, the throwing of her badge across the inside of the car, and then the burying of her head in her hands gave me a clear indication this was not a happy wife. To say she was frustrated was an understatement. By the third day, I could tell she was ready to quit.

I was devastated. My spouse is an extremely hard worker who succeeds in everything she does. Regretfully, she was promoted to manager and then left the company. Despite working there for several years and driving the store's vision center to record-breaking profit margins, she never received any training. She managed to make it, but only after months of excruciating frustration. Can you sympathize?

Finding someone, any person, to fill a leadership void is undoubtedly one of the most costly mistakes upper management can make. Frequently, when they need a manager, they take the easy route and, rather than doing their job and selecting the right person, they select anyone who demonstrates some knowledge or leadership. The selection process is typically based on a person's tenure or ability to perform exceptionally well at their particular task.

As in my wife's case, I've witnessed many exceptional workers being thrown into leadership roles without proper vetting and/or training. I've seen how this has resulted in costly mistakes within an organization or company, and the frustration that arises from both the leader and upper management has led to many of these leaders quitting or getting fired. This can happen when upper management resolves to use these two traits as their only identifiable criteria for choosing the right manager.

Someone humorously explained the process like this: Your boss summons you into the glorious throne room of his or her office. As you pass through the door, your innate sense of inferiority compels you to take off your shoes as you enter "the holy of holies." You feel a little nervous. As you kneel before his or her sacred desk, your boss reaches forth, and out from behind the desk, they pull out the infamous "Management Excalibur Sword." Your boss then chants an initiation rite. You're not sure what is said because it's said in another language known only to a select few - which is management, of course. As the rite ends, it's tapped off with the words, "You are now a manager. Go hither and yon and do it!" Just then, something hits you like a bolt of lightning; your body begins to pulsate, and you are now filled with all the great knowledge, wisdom, and experience you'11 ever need to become a successful leader of people! You have been instantaneously transformed and provided with strategies that would make a Harvard business professor green with envy. You are now a manager - a leader of people. Slowly, you stumble out of the boss's office, ready to go hither and yon and do it.

I know that seems a little dramatic, but I hope you get the idea. Is that what occurred to you? Probably not.

It is impossible to estimate the number of managers and leaders who have assumed leadership roles without the necessary training to develop into effective people managers. Leading a team to achieve optimal performance is a very different skill set from managing them.

Your title alone does not guarantee that you will lead your team effectively; even with a title like "manager," "supervisor," or "team leader," you are still not a great leader.

In numerous leadership conferences, I have used the following example:

Imagine that an F-16 fighter pilot led you through a brief initiation rite and then declared, "You are now officially an F-16 fighter pilot!" How confident would you feel about leaping into the cockpit and taking off? The truth is, you wouldn't do it. Of course, you would probably like to, but you know the dangers associated with an untrained professional flying an F-16 jet. Receiving the title of F-16 fighter pilot doesn't make someone an F-16 fighter pilot.

The people who truly bestow the title upon you are your team members! Although your supervisor or the organization may provide you with this authority initially, you won't be leading if your team refuses to follow your lead.

The fact that you aren't leading anything until your team is behind you makes me think of the guy who brashly proclaims, "I'm the leader!" before turning to see if anyone is following him. This reminds me of a quote by AlexandreLedru-Rollin that goes, "There go my people. I must find out where they are going so I can lead them."

Thinking about how much worse children might feel when they score low on an exam while knowing that others expect them to be smart can cause significant unwarranted pressure. Being told we are smart sets the expectation that we will behave smartly, which builds the desire to prove we are smart, even if we don't feel it.

The leader's expectation can become a burden when managers don't see themselves as leaders, especially for those new to management who already have reservations about their capabilities. Labeling managers as leaders has the same effect as telling kids they're brilliant.

In short, I worked for Renea, a vice president who joined the company from a different industry and lacked experience. Renea put a lot of pressure on herself to be a leader by claiming to be a leader of people, but from the perspective of her subordinates, she rarely demonstrated that she enjoyed her work.

Although she never explicitly said what it meant to be a leader, Renea implied that her subordinates should serve her. Although she wasn't a nasty person, she appeared to struggle to keep up her leadership persona. The organization no longer employs Renea.

When we have a fixed attitude, we tend to avoid challenging work, laugh at other people's foolishness, and then spread rumors to disparage others while suggesting that we are superior to them.

What if Susan had answered Rekia's question about how she felt and what she would do next rather than responding from a fixed mindset? Susan might have said in this case, "Even though I'm disappointed, I know that some supervisor positions will be available soon. When Orlando posts the next requisition, I'll be the first to apply!" Susan's response is far from feeling like a failure and stuck in a role.

Susan's response in the revised scenario stems from a growth mindset. When we approach life with this mindset, we think we can develop and improve our IQ, EQ, traits, abilities, and competencies. Thinking that adults can still grow leads to beliefs like: "I can still get smarter. I can learn to draw. I can take an art class to help." "Michael Jordan's remarkable achievements came from his dedication to practice and learning.

When we approach problems with a growth attitude, we work hard to find solutions, ask for a stretch assignment from our employer, ask a colleague for assistance, and acknowledge the efforts of others.

Here are six assertions I would like you to decide whether you agree with, partly agree with, disagree with, or disagree with.

Complimenting someone on their intelligence when they accomplish big things is not a good idea.

Hiring applicants who are fully qualified for positions makes more sense than hiring applicants who only partially match the essential qualifications.

Before trying again after a setback, I could feel demoralized or disheartened.

Certain professionals are born leaders.

My coworkers have a great deal of opportunity for performance improvement.

I occasionally envy a peer's advancement when I'm better qualified, even if I might not express it.

Either a fixed or developing mindset is represented by each sentence.

I'll give an example from Dweck's early years to clarify the first assertion from a growth mindset.[19]

Mrs. Wilson's sixth-grade class was different. She felt that her students' IQ determined their degree of intelligence and character: high IQ indicates goodness and low IQ indicates badness.

Mrs. Wilson took this idea a step further, seating her students according to their IQ scores, with the highest-scoring students at one end of the classroom and lower-scoring students at the other. Additionally, as Dweck explains, Mrs. Wilson only trusted the smartest students to carry special assignments, like the American flag. She reasoned that students with lower IQs couldn't be trusted to take notes to the principal's office and return on time. In her class, she changed the focus of education from learning to looking smart without looking foolish.

Region of Anticipation

One must possess leadership to successfully establish a business and win commercial competition. a strong leadership team can help businesses weather difficult times in a market where resources are scarcer. In times of crisis, turn things around and develop fresh competitive advantages.

Consequently, developing an exceptional leadership team and improving managers' leadership has

A good leadership development program should enhance participants' leadership and foster more loyalty and trust within the business to ensure that the investment in leadership is more than returned in practice. Naturally, most businesses are far from this "perfect" state for a variety of reasons, such as using the incorrect quality model or one that is too complex for assessment and development, employing the wrong evaluation techniques, overemphasizing the importance of training, and failing to consider the broad range of applications for various development modalities. It is easy to see that the selection of third-party agencies and the degree of leadership technical competence are the main causes of these issues.

We think that effective organizational support can be achieved by taking proactive measures in the following three areas:

Prioritize developing "professional" leaders.

What businesses must do is develop qualified leaders. Their occupation is a key characteristic. We can refer to them as "career leaders." They are not the same as philosophers, lone proprietors, or social activists. They are highly efficient and successful when it comes to putting strategies into practice, developing organizational skills, and establishing norms and order inside an organization. In addition to continuing to uphold the organization's order and core principles, they are better equipped to become experts in the structured division of labor. Because of this, businesses must determine early in the professional echelon or pool the conditions under which future career leaders may develop into "professional leaders" while fostering the professional leadership of future career leaders. These conditions include corporate culture (the organization's shared values and customs), policies, and procedures.

Without the components above of the company environment or the soil through which these values, rules, and processes are formed, it will be difficult for career leaders to make a difference.

Business companies may need to prioritize skilled executives for the long-term success of their commercial organizations. A single company may need just one or two talented entrepreneurs, specifically professional executives.

Reasonable involvement in stratification. Performance evaluation and intense training are the most popular methods of developing leaders. However, organizational interventions in regular work settings are more successful and long-lasting in enhancing cognitive abilities and teaching behavior change. If there is a "coach/mentor" in the workplace daily, they will remind others, oversee, provide feedback, have discussions, and their leadership will grow quickly. As a result, the performance will match the schedule.

Therefore, a company will build a strong leadership position if it can somehow lead every level of the leader into a "coach" or at least a coaching type leader who can practice daily layers of intervention. For the company to win the final success and the first opportunity in every competition.

Package for incentive mechanisms.

A leader's enduring allegiance is contingent upon the leadership aptitude that the organization fosters. Leadership development requires organizations to give talent the proper "treatment," "respect," and "sense of accomplishment" for them to "self-fulfill" within the organization. By establishing an appropriate pay scale, equity incentives to get "just and inspiring " treatment " can be considered. The primary sources of "respect" are the superior leaders' regular communications and acknowledging the company's basic principles.

Making decisions

An autocrat's capacity for sound decision-making is one of its greatest advantages. Given that the health and wellbeing of their patients are at risk, doctors must possess this skill. In actuality, those patients' lives are in danger occasionally. These circumstances make decision-making difficult, but autocratic doctors rise to the occasion. They can constantly make effective decisions because of their ability to analyze problems logically.

Making decisions is another essential skill for lawyers to safeguard their client's best interests. Autocratic lawyers benefit the persons they represent because they can rationally conclude from the evidence. Some people think authoritarian lawyers are arrogant, but their seeming haughtiness is confidence derived from careful situational analysis.

Guide

Individuals require plans of action, particularly when they are unclear about the best path of action. Uncertainty is eliminated and replaced with guidance by autocratic leaders. They offer the route that must be taken to achieve goals and objectives, which reduces tension for many people who are lost and in need of guidance.

College instructors who simultaneously function as academic counselors are instances of autocrats giving orders. They direct learners toward a successful college degree completion path. Because several courses are only given during certain times during the academic year, that path must be followed precisely. Because time, money, and effort are wasted when students are unaware of what to do to graduate, these teachers' autocratic leadership approaches are welcomed.

Response Time: Attorneys with an autocratic style recognize the need for promptness. They apply logic to decide whether to take actions that will best serve their clients. Sometimes, the situation calls for quick action; other times, it calls for waiting for opportunities or adjustments. A plan is required, regardless of how long it takes to respond. And this is the ideal situation for autocratic leadership philosophies.

Professors who are autocratic also recognize the importance of reaction time. They have self-imposed guidelines for assessing tasks and returning them to students, and they set tight deadlines for their pupils to turn in assignments. Students can concentrate on the subject matter of their assignments rather than the course structure because of this management approach, which keeps the classroom orderly.

Unrest

Emergency department physicians must work in turbulent environments. Patients feel intense pain in their bodies and fear for their lives. It is simple to understand why emergency rooms are chaotic when one considers the worry that the patient's loved ones are experiencing. To the best of their abilities, doctors must oversee their staff without being swayed by the irrational and occasionally bizarre behavior around them. Doctors with an autocratic style are the best leaders in emergencies because they make decisions based on facts rather than feelings.

Similarly, bankruptcy lawyers must act in the best interests of businesses facing challenging situations. Autocratic lawyers set the standard because they remain calm and assess problems without becoming emotionally involved. Additionally, they have a solid grasp of the circumstances and what lies ahead of them, thanks to reason and reasoning.

Many corporate executives also adopt an autocratic approach. While most of these executives are unknown to the general public, the following three well-known businessmen were autocrats as their companies expanded:

Ray Kroc

The California-founded McDonald Brothers restaurant empire would never have achieved global fame without Ray Kroc. Kroc elevated the brand and expanded it to heights that were previously unthinkable. He popularized fast food and created a blueprint for success that numerous other restaurant businesses have adopted.

Ray Kroc was an assertive leader, which many may not be aware of. He was a true despot because he thought McDonald's could only be as good as the individuals who worked there. His policies were clear-cut and uncomplicated and required compliance by all staff members in each restaurant. Franchisees who disregarded these guidelines lost their ability to conduct business under the recognizable golden arches.

Burger's creation using the "speedee service system" illustrates Kroc's authoritarian authority. This method, which the McDonald brothers first implemented, guaranteed that every hamburger would be the same regardless of the retailer. Strict limits are applied to customer service procedures, cooking temperatures, and hamburger portion sizes. Some franchise owners were not pleased with Kroc's implementation of a refund mechanism for customers who had to wait longer than five minutes for their orders.

Regarding financial success, Ray Kroc stands head and shoulders above the others. He established a dynasty, rose to fame, amassed a fortune much more than his requirements, and cleared the path for numerous other restaurateurs. He was one of history's most well-known autocratic business CEOs because of his uncompromising vision and dictatorial management style.

The Significance of Connections for Mental and Emotional Health

enhancing our ability to overcome obstacles in life. These connections provide a forum for empathetic communication, emotional expression, and a feeling of community, all of which help to reduce stress, anxiety, and loneliness. Furthermore, social interaction promotes the release of endorphins and oxytocin, two neurotransmitters linked to happiness and lowered stress levels. Understanding the crucial role of connection in our mental and emotional wellbeing is more necessary than ever in a society where loneliness and isolation are common. This emphasizes the need to foster and prioritize our social relationships for our health.

The Effect of Connections on Success in Both Personal and Professional Life

Connections greatly influence success in both the personal and professional spheres. Meaningful relationships with friends and family in our personal lives offer emotional support, motivation, and community—all vital for wellbeing and personal development. These connections add to our wellbeing and fulfillment while providing a safety net at trying times. Professionally speaking, networking and establishing relationships within one's field can lead to joint ventures, job chances, and mentorship opportunities. Through these relationships, information, ideas, and resources can be shared, promoting one's profession and fostering personal growth. Ultimately, one of the most important factors in determining success is cultivating and sustaining positive relationships in our personal and professional endeavors.

Getting Past Connection Barriers

While interacting with others can be a rewarding experience, many difficulties can be involved. These challenges can differ based on unique situations and character attributes, but some typical ones are as follows:

Communication walls: Several tactical methods must be used to break down communication walls. Talking alone is not enough for effective communication; one must actively and sympathetically listen. You may establish rapport and trust by paying close attention to what other people are saying so you can better grasp their needs and viewpoints. Using simple language free of jargon and excessive complexity can aid in simplifying messages. Body language and gestures are examples of nonverbal clues that should match what you say. When there are linguistic gaps, comprehension can be aided by patience and common, commonplace words. Additionally, you can ensure that you and your conversation partner are on the same page by seeking clarification and feedback during interactions. Putting these techniques into practice can reduce communication barriers and promote productive, insightful conversation.

Trust Issues: It may be difficult to connect and open up to new people if you've had bad experiences with betrayal or breach of trust. Breaking down barriers to trust is a delicate process that requires persistence, communication, and patience. Being transparent and truthful about your goals and behaviors is crucial for establishing or restoring trust in a relationship. Being transparent is essential to establishing credibility. Maintaining commitments and promises is another crucial tactic that demonstrates dependability. Actively and sympathetically listening to the other person's worries and emotions might assist in resolving underlying problems and anxieties impeding trust. Furthermore, establishing and upholding limits, taking responsibility for errors, and extending sincere apologies when required are all essential measures in breaking down barriers to trust. Rebuilding trust frequently takes time, and it's crucial to remember that while it can be readily betrayed, it takes a long time to repair.

Insecurity: It might be difficult to connect with people if one has low self-esteem and lacks confidence. It takes a journey towards self-acceptance and personal development to overcome insecure hurdles. Commence by acknowledging that no one is flawless and engaging in self-compassion exercises. Realistic goal-setting and acknowledging modest successes can increase one's sense of worth. Seek out the advice and encouragement of a therapist, spiritual advisor, family member, or other reliable source of support. You may increase your confidence by facing your worries and progressively moving beyond your comfort zone. A more positive self-image can also result from self-improvement and self-care practices like hobbies or prioritizing physical and mental health. Although breaking down barriers caused by insecurity takes time, you may cultivate more self-confidence and lessen the negative effects of insecurity on your relationships and personal and professional life by being determined and self-compassionate.

Time Restraints: Demands from the workplace and hectic schedules can make it difficult to find the time to establish and nurture relationships. It takes efficient time management and prioritization to overcome obstacles caused by time constraints. Determine which of your personal and professional responsibilities are the most crucial first. Make a to-do list or timetable that allows particular time slots for these priorities. When appropriate, learn to say no and assign responsibilities to others. Making the most of your free time can be facilitated by efficiency and productivity tools like Covey's Time Management System (see the Appendices) and time management applications. Establish limits, safeguard your private time, and don't be afraid to tell people what you can't do. Time constraints can be removed, and more time can be allocated to important relationships and activities by developing good time management skills and striking a healthy work-life balance.

The Application

Patients may start a session from the comfort of their homes if they have wearable motion-sensing gadgets and AR glasses. The motion sensors record every nuance of their movements as they work out. Real-time replication of these movements is done by the therapist using a comprehensive avatar of the patient. Through AR glasses, the patient can see the therapist superimposing proper movement patterns or highlighting regions that require repair.

For instance, the therapist can overlay a visual signal indicating the correct angle if a patient is not bending their knee to the desired angle during a certain exercise, and the patient can modify it accordingly.

The Advantages

Availability: With the elimination of travel requirements, therapy is now more accessible to a larger range of people.

Real-Time Feedback: Therapists can ensure workouts are performed correctly by providing instant feedback using motion-sensing devices.

Safety: The likelihood of injury during self-practice is greatly decreased by ensuring the postures and motions are right.

Data-Driven Insights: Since the motion-sensing technology stores data, therapists may monitor a patient's development in a quantifiable manner.

The Final Result

Patients reported that the online physical therapy sessions were just as successful as in-person sessions, if not more so. They had the self-assurance to practice independently since they felt capable of doing it correctly. On the other hand, because of the virtual model, therapists could treat more patients and provide flexible hours.

The Prospects

There are a ton of opportunities for virtual physical therapy to expand. These could include incorporating AI to recommend tailored workout plans depending on a patient's progress or creating virtual reality (VR) environments where patients can receive therapy in 'game-like' scenarios, increasing patient engagement throughout rehabilitation. Distance is no longer a barrier to effective treatment with the help of virtual physical therapy, an innovative combination of technology and healthcare.

Case Study 3: Chronic Disease Remote Patient Monitoring

Context

Continuous monitoring is necessary for chronic illnesses, including diabetes and heart problems. Diabetics' blood glucose variations or cardiac patients' irregular heartbeats may be warning signs of impending problems that call for immediate medical attention. In the past, patients would visit clinics regularly to have their conditions evaluated. However, what if ongoing, real-time surveillance could foresee emergencies?

The Problem

Patients may find it difficult to make frequent trips to clinics or hospitals for routine monitoring, particularly if they live in distant places or have mobility problems. Furthermore, significant abnormalities in vital statistics may go unnoticed during the interval between these visits. How can medical professionals close this gap and guarantee prompt interventions?

The Change

The combination of wearable technologies and cloud computing offered an answer. Patients could now be watched over in real-time, no matter where they happened to be.

The Application

Smart, easy-to-use wearables customized for each patient's condition were given to them. For example, cardiac patients had rhythm monitoring bands or patches, while diabetics used continuous glucose monitoring patches. These wearables monitored important metrics all the time.

The data was transferred in real-time to cloud servers via encrypted methods. Here, enormous volumes of data were evaluated by sophisticated algorithms that looked for patterns or abnormalities that would point to a problem. Alerts were immediately issued to the patient and the medical staff if any anomaly was found.

This method allowed for quick action and gathered a wealth of data that allowed medical professionals to better understand the course of the disease and customize treatment plans.

If you want to be respected by others, avoid being the person who always needs to comment on everything. Don't just make comments to make them. People who enjoy making reflex comments are much simpler to ignore, but the group will pay attention if someone who doesn't usually speak up suddenly does so and has something important to say.

After providing validation, express your ideas. It is insufficient to merely hear someone talk. Being an effective leader is demonstrating to your team that you value and understand what they have to say. To accomplish this, you must first affirm the other person's notion by restating it before contributing your viewpoint to the conversation. When people see that you value their opinions, they will be more receptive to your own. The first step towards being a competent leader will be improving communication skills. Now that you've established some groundwork discover what further abilities you'll need to develop into the kind of leader you've always desired to be.

Recast negative ideas

The advice to "make sure you're in the right frame of mind" may have crossed your ears. A frame is an idea, perspective, method, direction, or emphasis we apply to or attribute to an occurrence. It's the narrative we tell ourselves about a circumstance. Like a picture frame, the frame influences the interpretation of a picture or painting. For instance, a leader's frame might contribute energy that finds answers, promotes neutrality, or escalates a conflict or issue.

This illustrates a leader's frame: "An additional phase of workforce planning? I can never maintain optimism. Employee productivity is declining.

Things appear unattainable in this frame.

Reframing is a change of perspective, an alternative viewpoint or mindset, a different, more useful, and usually more expansive perspective that works better for you. In place of the preceding negative tone, the leader may have stated something like this: "Today as I deliver the news of further downsizing, I'll highlight what we are doing well and how downsizing is temporary—a setback that is a prelude to an even better future that we can all create together." This reinterpretation clarifies what is feasible and fruitful.

Here's a more illustration of a frame and reframe:

Frame: "I detest providing team members with helpful criticism. I don't want to cause them any pain since I care about them.

Reframe: "Offering discrete criticism empowers fellow team members to make decisions. They might or might not alter. If I keep my criticism to myself, people won't ever realize how ineffectual their actions could be.

Frames are the stories we tell ourselves to make sense of a certain circumstance. The phrases "That'll never work" or "That situation is impossible" instantly end things. Because we just don't know what will work, leaders need to shift their perspective to one that is more upbeat and enthusiastic. Nobody is aware of the location of the treasure! We must keep an open mind and not become closed to new information.

Harvard psychologist and happiness specialist Dan Gilbert claims that we are largely responsible for our happiness or dissatisfaction. It turns out that how we interpret the events in our lives affects how happy we are. We can choose the narrative we want to use to describe our experiences.2. Situations do not constrain us.

Viktor Frankl described the ability of the human mind to choose the final interpretation of experiences. A liberation he enjoyed while detained in Nazi Germany's extermination camps. Frankl was merely physically confined.

He used his human ability to control how that situation would impact him. Frankl stepped away from himself and discovered inner power, significance, richness, and depth in the middle of some of the most disgusting situations in the history of civilization. He became an inspiration as he started to assist others in reframing and finding significance in their pain. "Everything can be taken from a man except one thing," said Viktor Frankl, "the last of the human freedoms: to choose one's own way, one's attitude in any given set of circumstances."3.

Encourage and Demonstrate Happiness

All people must adopt positivity as a trait to withstand difficult circumstances. If you cannot maintain composure and hope throughout stressful situations, there is no way you can get through difficult circumstances.

Leaders must be resilient and optimistic in the face of a group catastrophe. It's your responsibility to keep people's spirits up so they will strive toward a solution. You have to live your life with positivity if you want to be a beacon of light. Maintaining your smile in the face of all attempting to pull you down is difficult. But you have to maintain your motivation to get through difficult situations. People around you will be motivated by your ability to be active if you can preserve your resilience. When everyone looks to the leader for guidance, the leader cannot afford to become distracted.

You must develop your mentality first to instill a positive attitude in your leadership. If you have given up on hope altogether, you cannot inspire hope in others. Recognize how to seek answers throughout a crisis. Learn to analyze critically and objectively without letting your emotions get in. Your perspective will shift once you begin to see the positive aspects of every circumstance. When people need the answers, you'll be able to locate them.

Utilizing mind-training techniques is an excellent method of practicing positivism. You can reassure yourself by saying affirmations to yourself. A lot of people record their voices saying encouraging and hopeful things. As an illustration, "I am a strong and capable leader. I'll work to resolve this issue and bring happiness to my people. Continue reading along these lines to hone your neurons' activity and vigor. You can record and listen to them before going to bed and when you wake up. Continually growing as an individual is the best method to improve the world. When you believe in yourself, you won't back down or give up in adversity.

Throughout history, the human species has encountered and conquered several obstacles. The words of courageous people shape every successful invention and every struggle for freedom. People can see through your optimism when you maintain hope even after everyone else has given up. Staying upbeat will sustain your energy and keep you from giving up altogether. Utilize it as a bulwark against self-doubt and insecurities.

Your aura should put others at ease if you want to be loved. Develop a personal equation-making relationship with the group you are leading. When they make mistakes, give them room to come to you. Above all, don't be scared to take constructive criticism.

You have to remember that failure is a part of being human. No great leader has ever achieved success without facing challenges and disappointments. It will be your capacity to rise from the ashes that will distinguish you. Act like a phoenix. You can always learn from the mistakes you make. When you succeed, pat yourself on the back. Never forget to believe in the world, yourself, and your people. If you are strong enough, you can motivate positive change worldwide.

Possess an Extended Vision

Most people are lost because they cannot see a way out of a challenging circumstance. Being able to envision the results of your work is essential for inspiring leadership.

People are more likely to believe in you when you have a clear vision for the future. Nobody likes to work for someone who isn't clear about what they want. Individuals on your team are likely to be uninspired and unenergetic if you exhibit hesitancy and doubt. You must maintain people's interest in a problem's solution. Using a vision, you can focus your energy on finding a solution to turn a difficult circumstance to your advantage. Don't let the likelihood of failure consume your attention.

Society leaders such as Martin Luther King articulated an idealized vision of a free society through their speeches. Their statements were infused with sincere faith and tenacity. The masses back leaders who are clear about what they seek. They cannot relate to them before they have faith in a leader's ability to transform the world.

Make your intentions and vision clear through your activities. Working closely together, you may encourage your staff to see the future as you do. Before they understand exactly what you intend to accomplish, they won't be able to find true inspiration in you. When you assign them duties without explaining what the final product will look like, workers are alienated from their jobs. To make those around you feel like they are a part of something amazing, share your vision with them.

In the absence of a long-term objective, your commitments will feel hollow. Think about your goals and communicate them often. As a result, people will remain engaged and enthusiastic about what lies ahead for them.

The essential qualities and attributes of effective leaders

There is no one-size-fits-all definition of leadership. There are many successful leaders, and their approaches might vary depending on their experiences, beliefs, and personalities. Nonetheless, there are a few qualities and attributes that effective leaders have in common that enable them to encourage, inspire, and lead their teams to success. This chapter will examine successful leaders' essential qualities and attributes and how to grow and improve them to become more effective leaders.

Visionary: A compelling and distinct vision for the future is a crucial characteristic of effective leaders. They can inspire and encourage their team by clearly communicating their vision and knowing where they want to go and how to get there. In addition, a competent leader cherishes the opinions and ideas of their team members and actively solicits their input before making choices.

Integrity is another quality that effective leaders must possess. Leaders who exhibit integrity, openness, and honesty gain the respect and trust of their group. They also foster an environment of accountability, in which everyone takes ownership of their choices and actions.

Integrity-driven leaders also set the bar for their team to meet, which promotes improved decision-making and a happier workplace.

Empathy: Effective leaders are also perceptive to the needs and emotions of those in their team. They understand that every individual is different and has various advantages and disadvantages. They strive to establish a solid, cordial rapport with every team member and customize their leadership and communication approaches to suit each individual. Empathic leaders also encourage a feeling of belonging and community, which promotes better teamwork and output.

Adaptability: Successful leaders can change and thrive in ever-shifting environments. They support their team's creativity and innovation and are adaptable and open-minded. Additionally, they understand that things won't always go as planned, and they're ready to adjust course and make adjustments as necessary. Adaptable leaders also show eagerness to learn and develop, which motivates their group to follow suit.

Resilience: The capacity to overcome obstacles and disappointments is a quality shared by successful leaders. Instead of viewing these experiences as setbacks or failures, they see them as chances for development and education.

They are tenacious and persistent, and they urge their team to continue in the face of obstacles. Leaders who show resilience also promote a culture of experimentation and risk-taking, which can lead to innovation and breakthroughs.

attributes that enable them to inspire, encourage, and direct their teams toward attaining their goals. Individuals can become effective leaders in any sector or industry by developing and enhancing these attributes. Visionary, integrity, empathy, adaptability. However, leadership is not static, requiring continuous learning and growth. By embracing these traits and committing to ongoing development, individuals can become leaders who inspire their teams to achieve great things.

Understanding your leadership style

Leadership is not just about having authority and making decisions; it is about inspiring others, building a shared vision, and empowering those around you to achieve their goals. One of the keys to being a successful leader is understanding your leadership style.

What is leadership style?

Leadership style refers to the unique way in which an individual leads their team or organization. It is a combination of personality traits, values, beliefs, and behaviors that define how a person interacts with others, makes decisions, and sets goals. There are many different types of leadership styles, each with strengths and weaknesses.

The importance of understanding your leadership style:

Conversely, by recognizing your weaknesses, you can improve them, making you a more effective leader.

Secondly, understanding your leadership style helps you communicate more effectively with your team.

Thirdly, understanding your leadership style helps you to make better decisions. When you understand your natural tendencies as a leader, you can make decisions that align with your values and views.

Assessing your leadership style:

Assessing your leadership style is critical in understanding yourself as a leader. Many different evaluation methods are available, which can allow you to identify your natural tendencies as a leader. Some prominent evaluation methods are the Myers-Briggs Type Indicator, the DISC evaluation, and the Leadership Compass.

Once you have completed an assessment, you may utilize the results to better understand your leadership strengths and shortcomings. For example, if you score high on the Myers-Briggs Type Indicator for the "thinking" area, you may focus more on logical analysis and less on emotions. Knowing this can assist you in communicating more successfully with team members who may have a more emotional approach to problem-solving.

"Core Competencies" against "Business Capabilities"

Understanding the distinction between "core competencies" and "business capabilities." These are two ideas that are frequently confused in popular business literature. Prahalad and Hame's 1990 definition states that a true core competency must satisfy each of the three previously listed requirements. However, many people will argue that their definition is very strict and that a corporation can still succeed by having other competencies, even if these are hard to measure. We will now enumerate eight of these competencies.

First competency: customer service

Maybe you can provide excellent customer service. For example, your call center may handle inquiries far faster and in greater volume than your rivals. Or maybe your staff training program is so good that it makes your salespeople intelligent, polite, and smiling service providers.

Competency #2: Delivery Time

Perhaps your pizza isn't the greatest in town. Is making, packaging, and delivering pizza in less than twenty minutes possible? When your clients start to get hungry, the speed variable might become more important than the taste variable.

Third Competency: Cost

Do you have such an effective supply chain or production line that you can offer the lowest-priced widgets in the area?

Competency #4: Buying Power Your biggest advantage may be your buying power if your business has been in operation for a while and you have been able to take a sizable portion of the market. Your capacity to purchase, relocate, store, and complete big orders has significant value.

Competency #5. Culture It's possible your office isn't the largest one on the street. However, you might have the most stylish one. Young brains may find an appealing business culture more tempting than a big office complex.

Additionally, the creative spark comes from young minds.

Competency #6: Collaborations

Even if you might not produce the best widgets in the business, you probably know someone who does. Gaining expertise in the nuanced psychological art of forming and preserving strategic alliances has benefits.

Competency #7: Quickness

One commonly mentioned obstacle is being little. However, it also offers benefits. Being the leader of a small business entails being an agile leader. A small, energetic workforce can quickly alter course as necessary. They can quickly retrain, retool, or refocus their efforts in response to market demands.

"A small ship is easier to steer than an ocean liner," goes the saying.

8. Design and Craftsmanship Competency

Maybe you're not able to produce goods as quickly as your rivals. Maybe you aren't able to construct as many. It's also possible that your charges are more than what your clients would prefer. The fact that you have a group of excellent industrial designers working in your back office could provide you with a competitive edge. Your items' aesthetic appeal alone may be sufficient to influence a potential customer's purchase decision if they sound better, feel more substantial, or appear better than your competitors. A piece of true craftsmanship may be worth much more when industrial manufacturing methods are the standard.

What, then, do you excel at?

Chances are, looking over the list above, you'll see a quality that your business or team can excel at. It doesn't matter to our issue at hand whether you refer to these qualities as "core competencies" or as simple as "business capabilities." Rather, our primary objective is to communicate to you—as a team leader—the immense value of critically evaluating your strengths and shortcomings to allocate your team's limited resources to the business characteristics that offer you a competitive edge. We'll go over a method (SWOT) in the following part that will assist in formalizing the process of determining your core skills.

Section Four

How to Become an Effective Leader

Taking on a leadership role might be intimidating. Even those with much training could experience difficulties taking on leadership roles. Here are some helpful hints and methods to help you lead effectively.

Have Enthusiasm

The quality that unites all outstanding leaders is passion. Working with someone who genuinely believes in the organization's aims could not be more encouraging or motivating. However, having passion alone won't cut it until people see your genuine concern for the tasks.

You can demonstrate your zeal in several ways. Use well-chosen language and the right tone to convey excitement for the tasks you must do. To give your staff the impression that you care about them as people, not just as worker bees, get to know them.

Mention the projects that you and your group will be working on optimistically. Share your plans and strategies to demonstrate to your team that you are giving the assignment your all. Your staff will share your passion when they realize that you are not afraid to get your hands dirty and get to work.

Take on a Leadership Role

One of the tenets of effective leadership that applies to everyone is that leaders lead by example. You need to be as motivated as your teams are if you want them to be productive. For instance, you should act the same way if you expect your team members to arrive at work promptly.

Don't make exceptions for yourself exclusively. Even though you have more duties than the others, they will be motivated to manage their time similarly if they see you can accomplish it.

Maintain Your Professionalism

Being a leader requires a lot of professionalism. There are various methods by which you might project professionalism. Here are a few instances.

Dress Appropriately: It's important to abide by the dress codes established by organizations. Ensure you follow these guidelines so the other team members understand how crucial it is to dress appropriately. Furthermore, it bolsters your credibility and shows that you take your work seriously.

Organise Effective Meetings To be friends with those they oversee is the goal of some leaders. Even though it could sound like a wonderful concept, managing a team in this manner might not be the most effective. Meetings can occasionally turn into social gatherings where little work gets done. The leader is too preoccupied with winning over everyone to discuss important issues.

Create an agenda to help you remain on task during the meeting and prevent this. Maintain control over the conversations while allowing others to voice their opinions. When the topic of conversation veers off course, carefully get it back on track. Statements like "That is an interesting story" are appropriate. As we were talking now, By doing this, you can ensure the meeting accomplishes its goals without giving your team members the impression that they were reprimanded.

Organise Effective Coaching Sessions: Coaching sessions assist you in addressing the behaviors of your team. This is your chance to highlight good work and refocus on any difficulties. However, you must first ensure that you have everything you need.

So that you don't have to leave or stop mid-coaching to acquire data, bring reports that you might need to refer to throughout the session. Additionally, you should locate a space where you and your team members may communicate without hindrances or disturbances.

Effective coaching sessions can reinforce the idea that each team member matters.

PART SEVEN

Honest Leadership in Practice

By exploring real-world case studies, this chapter takes us into the physical world of honest leadership. It offers a nuanced examination of successful implementations and priceless insights from candid leadership experiences. We begin by investigating the significant value of case studies in understanding the various uses of open-minded leadership concepts.

This chapter's first section highlights examples of effective implementation in the real world. A variety of situations are presented to executives to show how open communication has produced favorable organizational results. These case studies demonstrate how extreme openness can be applied in various settings and fields.

This chapter's last section focuses on the lessons that may be drawn from open leadership experiences. Leaders understand the difficulties faced, the tactics used, and the results attained by people and organizations dedicated to living radical honesty. For leaders pursuing their honest leadership pathways, this section offers insightful lessons to remember.

revealing how leaders overcame obstacles, promoted candid communication, and developed a climate of trust among their teams. These case studies are useful manuals for executives applying open-minded leadership concepts in their organizational environments.

An extensive analysis of how candid leadership affects team dynamics, organizational dynamics, and workplace culture is given to leaders. The case studies offer a sophisticated comprehension of the concrete benefits of adhering to radical candor principles.

The book skillfully integrates practical insights from frank leadership journeys, illuminating the transforming experiences of leaders negotiating the complexities of feedback, communication, and trust-building. This section provides leaders with practical tactics and insights to integrate honest leadership into their career paths.

In conclusion, this chapter explores case examples that highlight the practical implementation of honest leadership. Leaders can get valuable insights from successful implementations by analyzing and distillating lessons learned from real-world experiences. This process can take them toward promoting open communication, establishing trust, and enacting positive organizational change through radical honesty.

www.ingramcontent.com/pod-product-compliance
Lightning Source LLC
Chambersburg PA
CBHW071232210326
41597CB00016B/2022